AMONGST THE GRAPEVINES

Printed in Australia First Printing, 2023

ISBN 978-0-6457290-09

Amongst The Grapevines

MINNEY RICHANI

Minney Richani

Firstly and endlessly الحمدلله for without the grace of God, nothing is possible.

I acknowledge the first inhabitants, traditional custodians and rightful owners of this land, the Aboriginal and Torres Strait Islander people and pay my respects to elders past, present and emerging. I am honoured, privileged and grateful to be residing and writing on this land that is and always will be theirs. I invite you to acknowledge that Australia is stolen land and to heal country it must be returned to its rightful owners.

This book is dedicated to the children of the diaspora, those who were born onto constantly diverging paths, forced to navigate multidimensional identities on shifting grounds, through heavy clouds by twisting tongues that call more than one place home.

I am honoured and privileged to acknowledge the woman who both graced these pages with her presence and laced my identity with her essence. My dear sito Mayase, you are the heart that forever beats and gives life to the dar and to my Syria. I am in awe of this rhythm that you passed down to my mother, my sisters, myself, the generations of mystical and powerful women. We empower ourselves and those women around us through your being as a beacon that glows across time, place, culture and nature. For as long as grapevines continue to extend you will be loved, you will be appreciated, you will be known to the world.

My dear sister Rose. Amongst The Grapevines would have been only mere whispers without you, I have you to be eternally grateful for it becoming a reality. Our paths towards our purposes converged and to have you on this journey of creativity with me has encouraged all the possibilities to flow. I dedicate this book to you for your constant and ongoing support, for inspiring me, directing me, for sharing my vision and influencing my world and my writing. Thank you for terming the "inbetween" and for being a soul to navigate it with in this lifetime.

The cover of Amongst The Grapevines was illustrated by Zenah and Nezar. They combined their boundless talents to translate and celebrate my vision for the face of this collection. Thank you for your constant love, patience, feedback and support.

Mama and Baba no words in either language of mine can even touch the surface of my love and gratitude. You are my everything, everywhere and every moment. You did not only give me life but you did your best to push me to constantly live it, embrace it and grow with it. I fought you, I ignored you and at times I didn't appreciate you but God knows I've learned. The education, the freedom, the years and years of fish and chip shops, the thousands of kilometres to take me and drop me, the privacy, the trust, the world without expectations - you gave me, made this book.

Lastly and most bitter sweetly, I dedicate this book to my late grandfather, حياة Jido Merhij. You are missed, you are forever loved.

Contents

Syria, no not that Syria

I dream about a certain place. Sometimes I dream about this place constantly and sometimes months will go by before I revisit it. I slip away from the dream state into reality and refuse to open my eyes in hope that I could hold on to this glorified world within my subconscious just a little longer. Slowly, features of faces I had just seen become a blur. Buildings I had reconstructed from reality become rubble. All that would stay with me from these dreams was the sensations they had filled me with. For seven years I had been feeling as though Syria was somewhere I once visited in a dream. I missed my home country or background of origin or whatever it was they taught us to call it at school. I was in second grade the first time I was made aware of the distinction between the country one's parents were from and the country oneself is from.

"Where are you from?" Mrs. Gray had asked the class.

"I'm from Syria." I had answered with confidence when I was addressed.

"But Minass... where were you born?" Her eyes challenged.

"Umm over here... in Australia." I rubbed my hands on the rough carpet we were sitting on.

"That means you are Australian, Minass."

In second grade I was taught that I was Australian and that my country of origin was Australia. I loved Australia. It was my home, my family, my friends, the beach, Sizzler and everything else involved in the simple life of a seven-year old. I didn't remotely appreciate the way my teacher had dismissed a huge part of my identity. I felt heat rushing into my cheeks and lowered my head to hide my obvious discord. I didn't spend the rest of my life suffering from an identity crisis: I was content that I was just as Syrian as I was Australian.

Seven years ago things changed. When I wasn't dreaming I couldn't even be sure that I still knew Syria: the Syria that is my home. My identity was challenged after a crisis unfolded within Syria in November 2010. Before the crisis, people would notice my olive complexion and question my ethnicity. I would describe the tiny spec on the map beneath Turkey, above Lebanon and next to Iraq and receive blank faces. I would resort to, "An Arabic country within the Middle East, in Asia."

"Oh okay, never heard of it."

The media erupted with news of a civil, political, religious or an "American-agenda" driven war. Syria rolled off the tongues of news reporters, of politicians, of our customers who buy Chiko rolls and never leave Brisbane. Populations throughout the world spoke Syria's name and She didn't sound right in their mouths. I wanted desperately to snatch the word from them and defend Her. Yet I could no longer say Her name without the aftertaste of sadness. I have a friend who recently visited Lebanon and came back complaining, "too many Syrians in Lebanon now! They are overcrowding our villages! But you know what I mean - not your type, the Muslim ones."
"Where are you from?" People now ask.

"I'm from Australia." I cannot bear the looks of pity I receive when I say I'm Syrian. I felt detached from this Syria, as the two continents separated by the deep ocean were. So I revisited my mother's birthplace.

Swaida city is situated south of war-enveloped Syria and only twenty-five kilometres from the Jordanian border. Seven years into the Syrian conflict, Swaida city remains alive and appears to be external to the chaos that surrounds it. Swaida is neither under siege nor does its residents sleep to the sounds of bullets and explosions, yet faces are weary with affliction. From food to clothing and electricity, prices have increased by seven to ten times since prior to the war. Fuel is scarce and people are unwillingly making the decision to purchase ISIS-owned resources. Swaida has become residence to a large number of internally displaced Syrians who face similar struggles to refugees forced to flee the country. As for the city of Swaida, the biggest issue affecting its population is a social one and the war had mostly encouraged a dynamic of frustration. This frustration is a driving force to anywhere outside of Syria or at least away from their villages.

My time in Syria was spent in my mother's hometown, Orman. Orman is one of a hundred and forty-six villages located within the city of Swaida. The village is generally a poor place. Its people lead simple lives yet are majorly exposed to the elaboration of the West through the recent widespread usage of the internet and social media. This creates a sense of unease and frustration from the limitations the population becomes aware of in their own lives. The concept of the grass being greener on the other side predominately swells within adolescents who are driven to explore the world and its

تُفَضَّل عَمو

boundaries. Unlike their parents, their grandparents and if still alive their great-grandparents too, their minds know more than a world's population of 10,000, a world you can cover by foot in an hour. These adolescents that ache for more are young enough and are exposed too much for the society and culture to be embedded in them.

As an Australian of Syrian heritage, I am the one they look to when they wish to live a life other than their own. Growing up I continually invalidated their jealousy over my life, a life that involved belonging to two places and yet never completely being accepted by either. By wishing for my life they were wishing for an unsettled mind, a jet-lagged heart and a tongue that tripped over two incongruous languages. During this trip I realised two things: the world didn't know the real Syria and the Syrians I knew who lived there didn't appreciate Syria.

"Home is not a place, but a person." This effortless assemblage of words has appealed to many hearts. When one thinks of the word home, associations with comfort, memories, protection and even affection come to mind. Therefore it is no surprise that there is a cohesive level of interchangeability between a person and a sense of home. This poetic phrase presents a great compliment for the 'person' that becomes the subject riding this train of thought. In giving this compliment, so much is invested in the person receiving it. So much faith is placed in the person riding the train that they become the ones steering it. They are your home; their arms provide you with warmth and protection, the whisper of their voice feeds your soul, you drink in their touch and then, they are gone. They leave or they die or they disappear. They crash the train. The walls collapse. You are left starving. You are left homeless. My home is not a person. My life cannot be simplified by a trending phrase for poetic purposes and adversely complicated by those same words.

My home is not a person, it is a place. No amount of passing years, changing faces or corrupted values will alter my devoted attachment to it. I could roam the earth blind-folded yet the moment my leg rises, my foot extends and my toes curl in the gestation of entering the vicinity of the place so dear to my heart, every nerve within me would buzz with familiarity. I know the uneven and cracked paths as though they are the creases that line my palms. I've memorised the tangle of streets as though they replicate the veins twisting up my arms. Every road is as conversant to me as the arteries travelling to my heart. And my heart, no matter where I go, who I meet and what I do, I will always find within this place.

I was not born there, I was not shaped and moulded by its society, I was not taught by its educators, undermined by its inequitable system or restricted by its ludicrous boundaries. I was not born there but I grew there. I grew from unfamiliar faces that greeted me with smiles. Neighbours that welcomed me into their house like family heightened my spirits. Shops were not to sell you fruit or chocolate or glassware, they were to provide you with someone to have a great conversation with. Bliss was the way the village sang tunes of a bouncing ball, vocalised by children's laughter and harmonised by a breeze that cleansed your mind. The trotting sound of hooves nearing from a distance meant wind in your hair, exhilaration and a sore bottom as your grandfather directed you to circle the roundabout. The roundabout, the only roundabout the village had, was as significant as the circle of life itself.

History would have been taught on a blackboard enclosed within four walls but the chronicles were truly felt walking by the roundabout's centrepiece, gazing upon the windmill's infrastructure and looking into the wise old souls of our grandparents. On the uneasy rubble ground my shadow reflects that of a soldier whose spilled blood possibly runs through my veins. The English, the French, the Ottoman, and terrorists crossed these same grounds and were met with defeat. The victory meant freedom to look up at the night sky that, contrary to logic, was not the same sky seen from anywhere in the world. The haze enclosing constellations of stars was as visible as the smoke of a chimney. The stars themselves were so bright they could set two hearts ablaze. The scintillating moon promised to pass on everyone's prayers. Praying constantly escaped our lips but we did not pray for more, instead, we used God's name in appreciation of what we had. We settled for the lightness of a simple life as our backs settled against flat roofs with the heaviness of the sky falling on our eyelids.

My home is not a person, it is a place. This place is not a house but a house is its essence. This house is rooms that have borne witness death. It is ceilings that have observed the birth of life. It is a concrete floor that remembers the dancing feet of a happy bride. It is flowers blossoming through crevices watered by tears of travellers-to-be. It is herbs and spices and the echo of a hundred hungry bellies. It is a hose with patched holes being fitted by a hunched over old man. It is a sudden cascade of water soaking our shoes and a scarfed old woman oblivious to having caused it. My home is green and pink and orange. My home is happiness and chaos and sorrow. It is grape vines at six am with sunrise peeking through at my grandmother as she begins her day. My home is a playground in a mulberry tree with purple lips and stained hands. It is plum trees watered with love and dripping down our chins. It is a place that extends its welcome to the public; they come strangers and are farewelled with their private memories. This is my home. More importantly, this is our home.

"Home is not a place but a person." I'm not benighted by refusing the contribution of people in making a home momentous. After all, if I weren't the daughter of a man who returned to his country of origin to marry a woman who lived there, I wouldn't know this side of the world. If my grandfather's grandfather had not relocated from Palestine, this place would serve no purpose to me. If I didn't have over 60 family members attending my multiple birthday parties, I may have grown in age but I wouldn't have grown in love. I wouldn't love this home if I didn't experience the love I shared with its people. Visions of my home itself draped my memory, the people as a whole laced these drapes wonderfully and each and every individual was a blossomed flower embedded into the fabric.

My home is Syria, this Syria.

عنب من عريشة الدار

This Is Where The Mulberry Tree Used To Be

what is my childhood but a seed embedded into my soul extending branches that keep my memories whole the smell of mulberries fill my senses as tales of early days unfold in the shade of its bearing lengths and my adventures remain untold

I could not reach the gifts it bared so I relished in their sweet scent beneath the tree came melancholy and tears watered it with content beyond the tangle of branches the leaves sang tunes of our merriment now I picture gales throwing it about and waves of nostalgia hit me beyond extent

I never truly liked red and perhaps it reminded me that I couldn't return for falling mulberries my home my essence oh how much I do yearn for my dirt-covered toes my messy curls so young and so much did I learn I grew from those very roots so the tree and myself you cannot discern

Traversing Affairs

It was too late to have second thoughts now. Beside me, my mother's face mirrored my mixed feelings. Despite her weary brow and tired eyes, she smiled at me as her grip on my hand tightened.

"Don't worry sweetheart." Was she talking to me or convincing herself? It was both.

"Mama, everything will be fine." My heart dropped despite the steadiness of the flight. "Just imagine the moment you see Jido and Sito." Seeing my grandparents was the paramount reason she was heading to Syria. They were pivotal to her love for her home country.

"Oh God I can't wait, Noory." Her face softened a little.

It had been five years since the civil war in Syria had begun. Throughout this blood-shedding and heartbreaking period, the conflict had escalated and slowed at unpredictable moments but showed no signs of coming to an end. Whether it was safe or not to travel to Syria was never certain and our trip was justified by my auntie's friend's cousin's neighbor, "I swear my daughter life, is it vary safe, I come I go I see nothing, everyone happy, is very happy." Nonsense. With every different person you ask, you would get a different story based on a prediction from a religious text, a cousin in the army, or extremely dubious assumptions. Nevertheless, here we were, my mother and I, two and a half hours from landing in a war zone. This was the least of my worries. Yes, I could potentially die at any moment in Syria. My first breath of the air I so esoterically craved could be my last. I was aware of the overriding issues associated with Syria but my concerns of returning were more self-centered. Precisely one concern and it was all I could think of. It made the subtle hum of the plane's air conditioning overwhelming, pressuring my head into an unbearable ache. I was doing so well keeping him out of my life, refusing to allow myself to delve into the misery he stained the depth of my mind with. For God's sake, it had been eight months. Were eight months not enough to move on? It had been that long since I was in contact with him, the last time I heard his voice. The long-distance made sure it couldn't happen but I guess now that I was several hours from his front door, from the electricity his skin once caused, from the eyes I used to drown in, I slipped back to that daunting night two years ago.

That night I tried to sleep. The goal was to sleep, what the real challenge was, was to take my mind off my lying, cheating, now ex-boyfriend. It was like I was stuck in a maze and in the end no matter what path I took, there was only one exit; the exit that he stood in the centre of. No matter what I thought of in the end it went back to him and once I became tired of fighting him out of my mind, I just gave up. It was horrible. The moment that happened, image after image of his cheating ways raced through my head. Up until then, I hadn't wasted a single tear on him as I promised myself I would not. He was not worth me shedding a single drop of evidence of my intense pain over his betrayal. I felt so weak though and I had never struggled so hard to keep from crying. I managed not to do so but I had completely lost control of my heart and mind. All I felt was the strongest urge to stab myself and end the suffering. It wasn't just a thought, it was a plan, a disease that spread through my mind and demanded to take control. I vividly pictured myself going downstairs, opening the kitchen draw and clutching the knife. I saw the knife piercing through my layers of skin, through my organs and grazing my bones along the way. I pictured myself sitting on the ground, bleeding profusely, my eyes slowly becoming weaker, my breaths struggled before I completely collapsed onto the cold ground in silent death. I rolled out of my bed and I stood up. I walked out of my room feeling lifeless and flooding on the inside with tears. Instead of following my encouraging thoughts downstairs I walked into my parents' bedroom and sat on the ground against the foot-board of their bed. I sat there and just thought about them: my parents who have two children they love. Two children that complete the family they created and cherished together. I thought of them finding their only daughter perished on the kitchen floor as a result of her own doing. I then sat there and listened to my dad's snoring and for the first time in my life it sounded wonderful; like the most comforting sound my ears could know. I listened to my mother's slow familiar breathing and could almost feel it on my face from all the nights she tried to comfort my pains away. The longer I sat there the more at ease I felt, the more I realized the effects my suicidal actions would have and the more I didn't want the aftermath to be spilled upon my parents to stain the rest of their lives. That is exactly what saved my life that night and the significance of sitting on the carpet of my parents' bedroom is something I have since silently held onto forever.

My skin began to itch from beneath the surface and my fingers became numb. No, I was going too far with this. I am a successful lawyer who has her life together. I'm going to Syria for a holiday that I deserve. A mother-daughter trip that will be nothing but wonderful. I almost laughed out loud at how simple that was. Talking myself into mollification proved just as simple as allowing my mind to succumb to the darkness of despair. I was going to be okay. Seeing Amir will only give me the satisfaction of proving to myself that I am stronger than I think I am. "Oh my God mama... thirty-minutes!"

I beamed at my mother. "I wish we were going to see everyone at the airport like we used to."
"Everyone is waiting for us at Jido's house."

I slipped my fingers away from my mother's unfastened grip and settling my head back onto the uncomfortable headrest. I held my hands together in contemplation. I could never quite assemble the right thoughts to be able to wrap my head around the concept of two different places, on the same earth and persisting to exist at the same time, having so little in common. I didn't have the right words to illustrate a response to people's curiosity over how I could so completely belong to two contrasting places. Both Australia and Syria were my home and yet people in both countries, whether blatantly or secretly, perceived me as an outsider. Everyone was awaiting our arrival at my grandparent's house. "Everyone" included my aunties and uncles, my cousins and their children. Smiling, I knew they all thought of me as they thought of each other - I was family and I belonged in Syria. In that century-old house I was not an outsider. We... my father, mother, brother and I, were simply a piece of the larger puzzle, one that is constantly lost but bound to be found and returned, connecting and making the puzzle whole again. To almost everyone else in our village in Syria, we were just the rich kids, Australian by heart and Syrian only by name. As much as I told myself it didn't matter, a part of me, the part that longed to completely belong, was hurt by the dismissal.

"Chairs up and seatbelts on please." The flight attendant eyed me, as though she was repeating herself. And she could have been. My thoughts must have dulled out her American-accented voice.

"Sorry." It was instinctive of me, I didn't have much to be sorry about. Satisfied that I had obliged her request, the flight attendant continued on down the passage examining the rows of passengers.

"Agh I hate this part!"
"Do you wanna chewy?" My mother offered. "Na, no thank you my ears are fine."

Unwrapping an Extra my mother wasted no time throwing it into her mouth and chewing it vigorously. I knew the feeling, evidence that the body reacted to the change of pressure by attacking the ears. It was painful. I almost cried the one time I experienced it travelling interstate to Brisbane. Thankfully it was the only time I felt that pain. I wouldn't complain but it was unusual that the dropping pressure didn't have an effect on my arriving in Syria. The arrival element of the plane trip was still no more comforting knowing my ears were fine.
"Prepare for landing," the captain's voice sounded electronic over the speakers.

Filling my lungs with oxygen, I forced the pressure of the air out onto the internal surface of my chest. I stiffened my shoulders and clutched onto the armrests on either side of me until my knuckles gnawed at my skin. My heart raced as the plane shook coming to a landing. As the wheels hit the flat surface of the runway my head hit the back of the seat with a soft thud. Squeezing my eyes shut I waited for the seconds to pass as the plane finally slowed down and allowed my heartbeat to match its steady speed.

"Welcome to Damascus, the local time is 7:43 in the morning and the temperature is 23 degrees Celsius. If you are returning, welcome back home and if you're here on holiday, we hope you enjoy your stay."

Releasing the gulp of air I was using to stabilize my insides, I turned to my right, wasting no time, "what he should be saying is, 'I hope you escape the death sentence you've placed on your head.' HA."

"Noor!" My mother wasn't amused.

Thankfully our seats were the closest to the entrance of the plane, which also served as an exit since the size of it was so small. Of course by closest I mean right after the business and first-class seating areas. Carrying only our handbags and no hefty carry-on luggage for a change, we waddled behind the line of passengers heading towards the exit.

Taking my first step onto the industrial steel staircase and out of the plane, I was temporarily leaving a part of me behind. Still sitting on that plane seat was Noor, the ethnic Australian. For the next three months I was disowning her, I was leaving her behind, loosening my ties to Australia enough to just be. To freely indulge in the Syrian culture and remind myself of all the simple pleasures I fell in love with growing up. After almost three years, yet again I will be perceived as the foreign, privileged Syrian in the place I consider my home but I will no longer allow a society that doesn't understand me to define me.

Red Earth

birthing red earth rich with aging footsteps rich with smells that disperse themselves and settle on kitchen bench tops or on uneven concrete grounds or on Persian rugs also rich with vibrant colours poured out of now unrecognizable fingerprints from all the tracks that cross them all the tracks that have been crossed the moon was also once this rich but small lights imitated her in the 70s and now the village souls can't do without imitations potassium ate away layers of skin but it also filled the sky's view with lines of clean sheets back when the rich red earth found comfort beneath fingernails still thick winter blankets with shades and patterns matched with nothing warmed flat roofs after they were done warming the village souls seventy years later and vocal cords that are only a couple of numbers off from their station speak of kilometres on grey transport that clinks and clacks repetitively hearing as much as she does and our minds fill with a series of images as clear as the band of patterns that rises and falls and decorates the archives beneath I hope that all of her swollen bellies and what came after them listen when they hear her / here swollen red bodies permanently guard blue homes and as they empty themselves into them neighbouring bodies cough dense smoke into the winter inside homes winter smells like roasted chestnuts and potatoes and burnt olive branches in winter homes are lenient on dust and the Sahara desert finds parts of itself amongst these village souls that sometimes pile into the back of pick-up trucks to be thrown and caught like skidding pebbles along the road apple trees expose themselves to two degrees and reach out towards the only flames that don't hurt them riches still come but sometimes only the apple trees can still appreciate them when the clouds let them go to where they're needed most roots can sway this way and communicate with red earth and the red earth eases for a village soul to return to her roots ankles deep off balanced moved without moving nourished complete full of light full of her she'd been walking on deep water sometimes calm sometimes murky sometimes raging here clumsy stones the size of spread palms are built like elegance to meet generations to come but the more vessels these souls are carried by the less rich they become and sometimes they weep but slowly as slow as the droplets of fuel that the wejaq catches desperately because it's easier to shiver softly for an extra day or two snow like bullets that pierce the chilled air and sends children to their homes to warm the blankets in homes where they find their parents huddled around the defeated metal stove filled with nothing but air that whispers apologies in homes with ovens filled with mismatched bowls of makdoos and zaatar and laban that could last a few more days hardened bread that survives in quiet fridges is enough the hum of electricity lights up sets of eyes in unison maybe it will last a few hours this time

The Mohamad Boys

You don't really think of electricity as a sound needing to be heard. You wouldn't think of it as bringing to life a static orchestra with one instrument at a time to echo throughout a home. Every four hours, we welcomed the hum that would wake the fridge from hibernation and rescue the produce from summer temperatures. Our eyes were relieved as yellow pools that hugged the walls replaced white lights. Showers could be planned as the water heater groaned and angry molecules kicked the inside of the metal body with impressive thuds. Our phones would go from being in our hands to being plugged into walls via adapters that accommodated to two parallel punctures. This would be our second home together since our wedding less than a month ago. The pattern of electricity was not only a shared aspect of the two homes, but a constant variable across all the homes within the village. Two hours of electricity and four hours of feeling deprived.

"Majde." In the mornings his name was a soft whisper and vowels were stretched out in tunes. A groan escaped his parting lips as I continued to tap his nose.

"Good Morning Manoos." I caught his smile before the sheets covered his humility. Our relationship had been developing over two years. For most of the two years, we relied on static phone lines that required dialling country and area codes. They also required patience through lack of electricity or lack of reliable reception. For some of the two years, the privilege of owning an Australian passport had me visiting Majde in Syria. My last visit turned into a wedding, then into a shared life together. But this wouldn't end my travelling between Syria and Australia.

"Up, up." I now patted the blanket where I assumed his head was.

A muffled, "Yallah."

"I'm going to get the mattee ready, yallah follow me."

Our current home was my family's home in Orman. My family had travelled back to Australia after the wedding and we moved into their home. We were living in an apartment that felt like living within strips of an undeveloped film. It was noon by the time we were sitting cross-legged on the Persian carpet in the living room. Sunlight poured out of the windows metres above us. Majde liked his mattee sweet, so sweet that I had to bury the green beneath white crystals. The house was silent, as it had been all night so it was a relief when the orchestra re-joined us as Majde raised the bambeeja to his lips. The filtering straw slipped out of his mouth and, in hurried movements, Majde claimed the good phone charger.

Looking up from my phone, I saw the dark depths beneath Majde's eyes and a complexion that resembled leftover turmeric yoghurt. I knew he had also discovered what suddenly stained my home screen. Facebook, Instagram, Whatsapp conversations from family members, all bled of a massacre that occurred within two villages, only an hour away from Orman. Our fingers worked our screens profusely to try to make sense of what happened, and yet our minds failed to latch on to any sense. It was 5AM on a Monday when ISIS invaded the villages of Shbiki and Rami. Men, women and children were not spared gruesome deaths. Rapidly, this news spread across the villages, across the country and escaped the borders of Syria.

The Mohamad Boys, they stand there at a makeshift checkpoint at the beginning of the village. There, being right in front of my family's home. A total of twenty-five gunshots have echoed across an eerily quiet night and trembled through villagers' nerves. On the first occasion my heart slightly stammered but I continued to make dinner. I trapped the steam of the complete ingredients when my phone began to vibrate against the kitchen bench. My mother in-law called to ask about her son's whereabouts. Her voice was riddled with worry. Her son, my husband, was not home. I assured her it was nothing and that it was probably alcohol-fuelled bullets to the sky. Probably. I said a hurried goodbye and called Majde.

Since the events of Shbiki and Rami, a wave of fear and inherited bravery had swept across the city of Swaida and all of its corresponding villages. Many young and untrained men spilled into the two villages soon after the ISIS attacks. Some were met with their last pulse of courage and others walked away as living heroes. Many ISIS members had been defeated and others escaped into rugged land. In the weeks following the tragedy, Orman fell into a state of apprehension. Weapons invaded most homes and villagers mentally prepared themselves for defence against ISIS. Various armed groups across Swaida did the same, yet Syria was a war-torn country with no laws to protect the oppressed and no laws to prevent the oppressors. Now, weapons were in the hands of both.

My heart dropped when I heard Majde's voice, a detached sentence of breaths and whispered words.

"Bye, bye," he hurried.

I was mid-sentence and desperate to latch onto meaning. The phone line had just died when Majde walked through the door. I called his mother to tell her he was home and safe. Again, gunshots sounded followed by voices. Raised voices. Low-pitched growling with high-pitched releases. One voice, two voices. They became clearer and more daring. The west end of the village rose and leaned their ears to the nearest windows and doors.

Insults, red throats, corrupted minds. This wasn't ISIS. This was the group of armed civilians who chose to stay up all night at a checkpoint to guard the village. These were the men to protect and warn us of any threats. They were drunk. Threatening. From what we made of the yelling and the numerous phone calls we received, there was a reason behind the disturbance. These men were previously paid an amount to ensure their services. This questionable payment came from our neighbour with the looming dark fortress for a home. One of these men was attacking our neighbour's front gate. He demanded money and he raged about having to guard the checkpoint alone. The drunken stupor was continuously interrupted by the second voice in a failed attempt to calm him. Nawaf and Fares Mohamad were becoming recurrent names in the village and tied to their names were rumours of illegal trades, alcoholism, vandalism and a family that was quickly dissociating from them. The Mohamad boys.

The dramatic change in atmosphere within Orman placed strain on my relationship with Majde. He wanted to purchase a weapon and I wanted otherwise. My awareness of the outside world and my recent experiences in this one made me more adamant towards my viewpoint. Majde's response was variations of, "what if ISIS break into this house and threaten your life, do you want me to just watch?" In the end he did what everybody else was doing. He joined the men on night errands and my heart was hung from the frame of the door until he returned. When months had passed and ISIS was a dissolved threat, the weapons still remained and threats manifested. Majde and I shared a third home in Syria in the heart of Swaida city. The pattern of electricity was different there; it was the tune of a single harp. We had found an impenetrable sanctuary within a city of intermittent chaos. This sanctuary was enough for the two of us, but Majde's family and friends remained in Orman, and he was constantly pulled to it.

Anas Abou-Hamra. I never saw this man wearing anything but a camouflage uniform. He talked enthusiastically and seemed to be the hero of whatever story he was fabricating. He was related to my grandfather and visited him often. Sometimes he would attend to an electrical issue and other times his lies would cause too much static in the room. Though, it was his sons' names that struck electricity throughout the village.

It was still odd waking up in Majde's parent's bedroom. It was odd to be sleeping in their home and not our apartment in Swaida. I was okay with it sometimes. I was okay with it this time enough to wake Majde with soft kisses and a smile. Here, we rarely left the bedroom together, like teenagers in a secret romance, not wanting to be caught in the room of the host at a house party. I walked out of the room and the hum of electricity was harmonised by my mother in-law's soft voice. Rarely did something perturb her state of calmness and this was mostly convenient considering the recurrent calamities.

"Did you open Facebook?"

"Why what happened?"

"Okay, it's Fares Mohamad. He's been killed." Majde and his mother fell silent. I stood wide-eyed, afraid to react. "Nawaf is in the hospital, he's been shot and doesn't know about Fares's death."

Majde knew them well; well enough to keep his distance from them yet distances in this village were brief. The Mohamad boys were related to my father in-law. They were also his neighbours who lived three houses down the road. That was where Majde's father now was.

"What happened? Who did this? Are you sure this is real?"

Fares Mohamad was a father of five, raising a disabled eldest son with his young wife. He would travel to the capital to make a living enough to maintain the level of poverty his family was accustomed to. The capital also allowed him to place guilt-free distance between himself and his brother. Fares put aside his hesitations yesterday and returned to the village with his family. He returned for the last time. He would defy sanity to defend his brother for the last time.

"I have your payment, meet me at my place.

"Nawaf didn't hesitate before flinging himself onto his motorbike, there was nothing he couldn't do while intoxicated. He headed towards the roundabout in the centre of the village with a renewed sense of recompense.

"Where is it?" Nawaf remained standing.

"I have it, but I don't have it with me right now."

There was a shuffle in the corridor and Nawaf glimpsed a shadow before it escaped the light.

With a fist full of Ashraf's tee-shirt he threatened, "I will kill you."

Nawaf re-joined the road that was swept with shameless moonlight, leaving behind the dust of the Sahara desert. In the house the shadow emerged from the corridor as Ashraf's wife. The night shook and she muffled her gasp in her hand. Ashraf stood in front of his home and as Nawaf's body fell to the ground he released the pistol's trigger.

Ashraf and Adil stood in a guarded stance at the roundabout. Nawaf was rushed to hospital and Fares rushed to the roundabout where he thought his brother still was. Fares and his older brother, unarmed, reached the roundabout. They found no Nawaf and instead were met with gunshots that bounced off the tar.

Fares seared in pain and reached for his leg.

His older brother ushered him back into the car.

Fares approached the car.

Fares knelt into the car.

He knew his thoughts were his last, yet even they were interrupted as Adil leered over Fares and sent a bullet through them.

The day before Majde and I were to travel back to Australia, a treaty was being pre-pared to be signed by the Mohamad and Abou Hamra family. Nawaf was out of hospital and now knew of his brother's murder. He was under scrutiny, expected to avenge his brother's death. The Abou Hamra boys had fled the country. Majde and I were leaving Syria, but there were things we couldn't leave behind.

Petals That Bleed

roses are red and so is the trickling of blood a sprinkle of sugar a sprinkle of bullets kills by the hundred violets are actually purple but these beatings are blue water them with tears like salt rubbing on an open wound

We Never Ate Cereal

gunshots like trying not to focus on the sound of cereal in your mouth on an early Monday morning with something in your veins saying it didn't really happen followed by a single echo that brings veins back together because there was nothing that followed

Spoils Of War

wooden doors seizure against frames and pink curtains breathe against a world separated by black mesh screens and I can hear an oversized vehicle leaving the village to
benefit from the black market and I can hear my husband whispering in prayer or to
read another "urgent" Facebook post that takes the urgency out of moments we have
together on the couch where he now sits alone with his rifle with its holy ribbon tied
tight against its handle as though it would make handling its use any more honourable
as though suggesting to visit a Mazar would make us people of God as though God is
content with us not speaking in love

Khawati Hayati

all five of them wore black and the ashes within the wood-fired stove from last winter barricaded their eyes yet overwhelmed with pain they leaked of something distant like the suppressed rain that the soft red ground yearns for but everything they mourned they hid poorly within the white of their eyes like sprinkling salt on snow until their view of the world dissipated everything evil until they no longer knew evil enough to avoid it

Mama's Hair Still Curls,
Mine Doesn't

they used to make doors not just the colour of wood but of actual wood with an asymmetric pattern too uncomfortable for eyes to be accustomed to and customs were never challenged with awareness when ignorance was made out to be so beautiful / I had never and I have never seen houses of deep blue of volcano blue of romantic evening blue suffocating red earth with its expensive heaviness with ten years two pregnant stomachs red lines carried by an abdomen that the grill carried / purple encasing the tears that didn't escape rich curls that black hair turned grey strands weary that a grey moustache rose and fell to invalidate it all but another ten years made this place home and made this place a sanctuary for poor newly weds from rich homes and my curls are now missed from either over-bleaching or travelling back to grills that create all sorts of different red lines

Location Location

location location

for lack of houses for lack of hours for allowance for options for views this bloody stream queasy but red is pretty or "fireworks" uneasy on the heart adaptable to the ears triple the price and a store on the corner price of gold for a packet of rice school is free the teachers are nice it's ceiling free though and fear comes through with the soft breeze nature there's one tree nearby and in winter life or death to kill the tree and your neighbor who also didn't want to freeze it's just a short walk to the bakery five hours in line your temper risen oh you don't know how to bribe there's no bread didn't you listen buy this car you can't afford go for spins in the street so you don't get bored get cruel on your tank then desert your vehicle on the waiting list thirty-eight days for a refuel

allocation for relocation

for lack of language no name no identity no lack of anguish a number on the scale between desert and salvage for fatal or unsafe you probably don't want to leave but you must cave in to flee for safety onto the borders or beyond the shores options options how lucky you are that all you know will be distant and far lucky for the cameras in your face between Hungary and Austria and the new names your new race will foster; immigrant and refugee hungry for settlement so the media kicks you in the stomach for situation embellishment glad they got that footage so people in America can feel sad and then invalidate the message that it's actually happening not in their back yard or in their life down the track so their mind discards it and they turn their back on humanity on faces of women and children who do not cry because they've faced death and the heat of torture that runs their tears dry collocation collocation

in dreamless sleeps you utter words spoken and voices unheard birds still sing tunes and you see their free silhouette through the thin of the tent your country is in ruins and you thank Germany for taking you in / you flood their streets and it weighs heavy on you a burden you carry in one arm and your child in the other you wonder if Australia has space and no harm so you speak and you ask in broken letters and no grammar / someone must hear and address the matter temporary stay for the minority for no Muslims but the latter for the few or the none that don't cause them uncomfortable chatter not for the millions of your brothers and sisters that outside the war still suffer cuts and blisters just for the minority that danger is not acquainted with but they will still give lashes of racist statements as though you do not hear because you're a world away and looking for peace in their country is what they fear

"Say Something in Arabic"

in the language I think you request with fascination for me to speak in my trembling mother tongue when my western home directs the words to collect with dust and tears at the back of my throat while you ask of me to pronounce heavy letters that only a dense history teaches and that forgotten past lives imbed as braille onto my soul but I no longer speak Arabic I speak the language that pleads for salvation I speak the language that thirst makes difficult on my lips I attach the letters together with tired hope and I watch my words within the aged creases of young faces I assemble my words delicately as I think of fragile hearts my pronunciations echo through demolished homes my vocal chords strain with war while you ask of me to say hello in Arabic but all that my mouth helplessly allows is please in Syrian

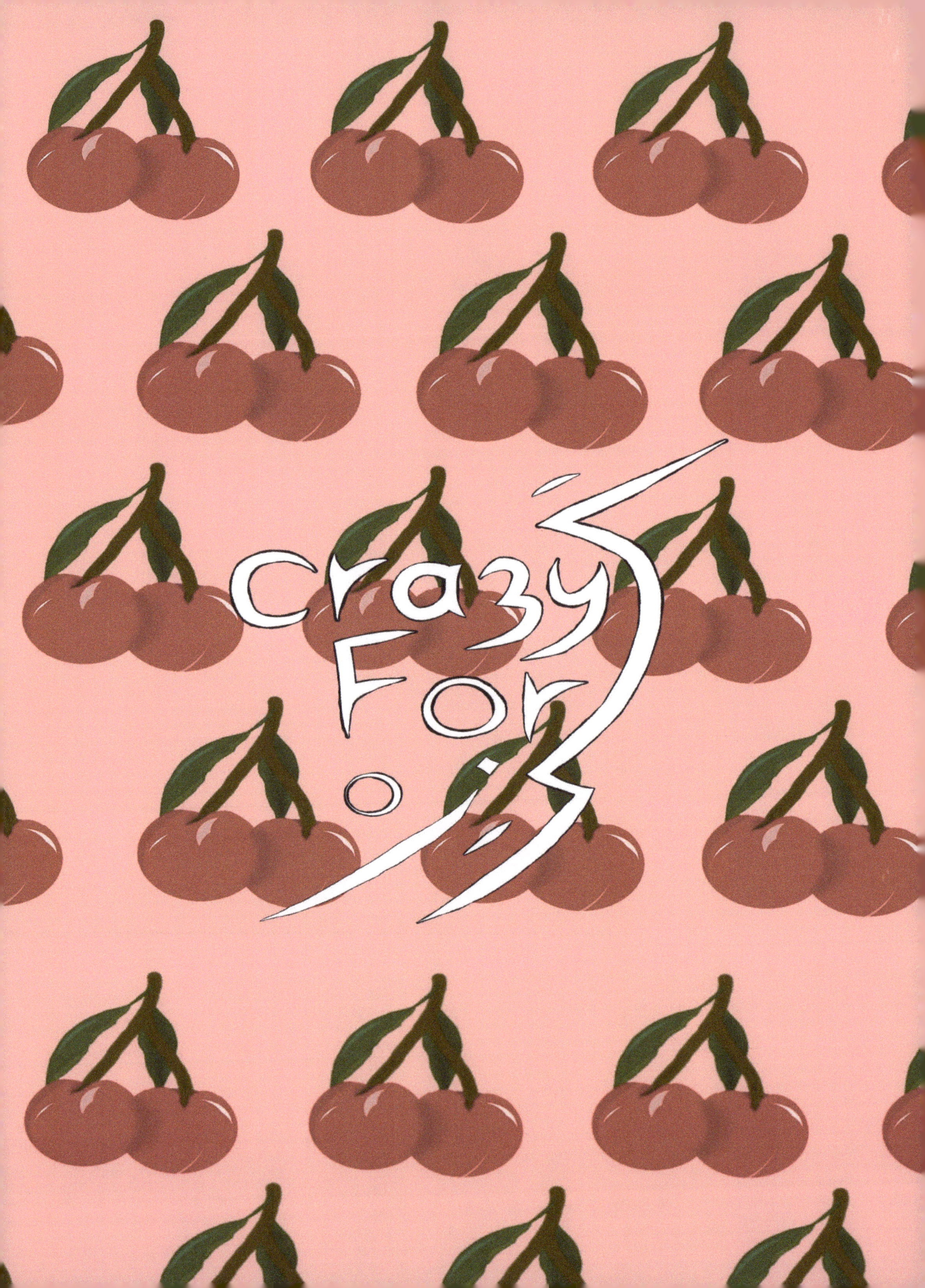
crazy
For

Betrayal

it eats at my soul the betrayal I've committed it doesn't creep through my senses under the vulnerable blanket of the night neither does it startle me as it flutters in through the blinds with the morning waves of sunlight it hangs heavy around me like the dust in the air aching my lungs with every intake of breath and settling on me like a thick second layer of skin its intensity rises with my chest and only falls to sink into the pit of my stomach like an untreated cancer that continues to swell it coats my lashes and every blink of my eyelids is heavy lagging my vision and flickering like an old motion picture film where I'm the villain the monster the betrayal hiding behind a mask of safety and comfort my hands raised against a thin wall of glass staining it with dripping crimson that runs through my veins yet I bleed none as though purposely wearing glasses I do not need blurring my vision whilst my head is clear with dread and guilt I do nothing and feel everything as I betray my own country

Empty Cups

I'll have tea(r) for one please sitting at a table for four pouring into each empty seat versions of the past which phalerate in their mockery of pain drinking in bittersweet only to choke on salty streams half-cup empty half-cup full pointless repetitions turns the full cup cold upside down I purposely scatter shards of porcelain that linger in the air breathing in reverse carbon dioxide sterilising the seeds within my lungs / quiescence in the lack of flow in my life developing a mellifluous ringing in my ears simultaneous with the clatter of porcelain on floor and three faces are staring through me deceased yet vivid in my mind and there is no comfort in knowing they can't reach me no holding back cries yet my throat is voluptuous with pain / tea(r) for one please but I'm not only crying for me

Breathing Sails

I'm just trying to breathe while time is trusting me to leave a bloody crust on my grief / healing wounds you can't see peeling layers of afternoon and setting the evening free to ignite a starry sky forgetting the heaving and the fight to get by under the dull light of the moon thunder strikes waves onto the hull of the oversized spoon / if the sea were to hold our graves it would be soon / if numbness were an art to master the mess in my head would become a silenced disaster the cold and the stress would duel to kill me faster but if we reached the steady shore of foreign land and beseeched the ready strangers for a helping hand exchanging our home soil for travelling sand that will keep changing tone unraveling never ending challenges would it be enough? would safety and security in a country that isn't ours make us wish to ungratefully turn back the hours not burn our loyalty and flee an attack but hold our ground and sing our pride make a sound to bring Syria back and undivided? I could do more than just try to breathe

Labels

I am from the middle from the east a country cast aside the ground deteriorates at my feet I have a homeland and a home from which I must flee my heart is grounded in the fields from the sweat sack on my back all these planted seeds my own seed flesh and blood my son I buried and watered with tears I've wrinkled I've aged I've suffered a million days in only these past six years four walls I had with health and warmth and I thanked God without greed now water does not run food rots in my mouth and it's a miracle to not bleed I want my country I cherish the was and do not want to leave so understand when bullets and bombs become an ongoing symphony my only choice is to look to the seas we want safety we want survival we are humans we are people we matter and we are what you label refugees

Motreb

what is the cost of a life? not a single self-aware person would say anything but price-less but spend two hundred dollars to invest in your foolishness and you have killed a family of six don't write about it she says don't express your utter disgust but the father is on the run but the mother could only carry two children across the border but the eldest joined ISIS because he couldn't survive withdrawals but the ten year old son is still roaming the homeland and it's not a case of saving up to get out of a shit hole when there's nothing to save except a spot on the street to retire from the constant reminder of death and that the scent of it so much sweeter than the plucked shells raining down meer metres away to find an excuse to close his eyes for anything but the dust of his demolished house which serves a reason to use his grated skin as an excuse to cry and you sit here with your twenty-year betrayal finding everything and anything to fill the void of "sympathy" to spend your two hundred dollars because your conscious weighs you down and instead of picking the Syrian child up you lift your own mood

New Year 2016

sparkle sparkle you twirl around absently blinded by your own glow bushy eyebrows raised and thoughts lost in them as the efforts are too much moving forward at a pace so speedy you lose track of why you came here in the first place I only wish to pop this bubble but the layers are too much and I ask for freedom of thought yet you wrap your ignorance around me with a soft blanket and outside it's too cold and the numbness of the weather reaches deep within me the snow refuses to settle on the ground as their ideas refuse to settle within my mind yet here I am smiling and dancing with the soldier that holds his position at a barrier that protects nothing but his pocket and the gold adorned beneath his collar is brighter than the sun that rises each day and the hungry child sins a hundred times before his waking hour will the bed he laid in the night become a grave buried beneath futile war?

كُلُّ عَامٍ وَأَنْتُمْ بِخَيْرٍ

Modern History

greenery that doesn't exist fills each corner of your bedroom and sucks the life out of your unconscious bodies greenery that is too bright for your dull eyes haunts your dreams in the night / water your silk pillows and dream of harsher days ruin your cashmere pajamas and attach yourself to them as though they're the only things you have wake the hell up and look out your window to your neighbour who cannot breathe look into their eyes as they choke over the loss of the infant they couldn't feed look at their blue skin that the Middle Eastern winter didn't forsake / can you count how many graves barricade the far form simple life they're living? now give yourself a round of applause your ignorance is modern history

Kite

stripes black and green white and red edges and corners not quite a triangle but pointed somewhere before it got stuck attached and controlled yet it was wild and free before it got captured it became detached freed of dominion a fine line between that and freedom a fine line between the end and what's not to come nothing without nature and yet nature opposed coming in the way of direction of following the wind that travels aimlessly unintentional resistance swaying and swaying with force to either remain or rejoin the whistle of nothingness

Be Somebody

hello nobody can I reach out and grab the sun? can I teach you a thing or two about being warm? there are mirrors on the other side and that's why I never turn around I just bend my neck a little backwards and pretend that I enjoy seeing through all the thick lashes of those that bleed the sun / blue veins turned red when they should be the colour of the rays hello nobody, can I steer you out of your own way? can I hear you read the bible? and have you crucify your unjustified greys to praise the living while the dead are dreading to meet us again worship the sun again for exposing you / rebuild your idols and hide in their shade as your little girl hides in the darkness of your pupil she explores the history on rubbled floor not allowing the red balloon to drop heart shaped innocence her favourite colour isn't pink and she wears it lovingly hello nobody why are your knees clashing together? in sync to the dancing flames rising ahead why are you shaking your shoulders? to sober your angels they haven't registered anything yet they're sending silver change your way high beams on and I'm dueling the sun / let me see the naked sky please and learn to ask me if I'm okay we all need to swallow up warmth whole

Sito

one two three who the hell am I speaking as if I have it all and sipping it down slowly I'm only one gulp in and it's been an hour making others feel responsible for happiness and I'm laughing I'm laughing number four not including me the fourth living generation from the top "the screen is too small I can't see it" and technology is too large it blinds you / expanding minds reduced to conformity wrapped in your ethnicity, reduced to your ethnicity I know you're not convinced he's explaining buttons and software you're as confused as the ageing lines on your face the cup has been thrown out and the rim lined with sobriety I'm staring at it with a drunk mindset replicated by those around me / five number five is the wisest carrying around eighty one years on her back thirty-five grandchildren not including the great-grandchildren and you hit me with feminism and the pride almost brings me to tears and the price of it is ignorance you were born in the wrong era I was born in the right place longing for the wrong people swimming with the tide to not be seen yet you're all beneath the surface and I'm breathing my own space because I'm an individual and your individuality is your race

White Words

snatching her name from mouths that bounce her letters on marshmallow tongues and undermine her wounds by filling her flowing Damascene rose with the rubble of twin towers

Martyr

the sun of whom didn't rise today from the north east west or south region how many years are in the strength of his jawline the speed of his feet the sun of whom whose mother was forced to wear shades for the rest of her living death whose father's face blackened by shaded light and suppressed tears / with the rising son I wake to spend the morning slowly withdrawing the knife within my chest to hear that the sun that is you rose another day

A Tourist In My Village

I think it's time to speak what's on my mind because I feel it within each brain cell vibrating throughout my being and there's no way of defining the person I should be because there is a limit and that limit is my personality they're all around me pressuring restriction and encouraging a sanity that compromises everything I could potentially be; the closest ties I have threaten to creep up my body and adorn my neck insensitively they all think they mean well but there's no way to understand burns that heal so well with painful absence painted faces and clothes that fit too well for poverty enveloped homes that drown in liquor and marijuana that cause you to choke on grains of rice and you measure the dollar by the price of zucchini your most hated choice of diet becomes what you crave the most and the craze turns you into all the evil that you invite / you tell me to look at your wounds yet they are not external and I tell you to look to your sister but your eyes bleed from the tears you refuse to associate with your oppressor you sing tunes in harmony with the enemy you fear to dissociate with dancing not with the devil but to the tunes of a child's screams and the symphony of bullets nothing pierces your skin yet the sound of deep depression echoes within you I am a traveller yet I am one of you so acknowledge me as a person and acknowledge yourself as an individual because you are not the society you live in and the power that shapes your path is not stronger than the power within you do not look at me as though I am practicing foreign ways look at me as though I am you and be proud

Haram

married three times divorced clearly she's not good enough "just so embarrassing" says her step-niece who hasn't seen her in years / she's selling the roof's wooden frames to get herself and her mother through the summer / prices burn in their throats and they chew their food too much they collect tears in their pockets where dust stays afloat chipped nose and darting eyes that don't travel too far transfer the kettle on the stove to the rusting tray on the ethnic carpet in the living room she just bent a little I caught a glimpse of bulging body caught in traveling jeans my grandfather's half-sister had no door to her room and I swayed a little too far standing in the kitchen "just disgusting"

he used to lay a hand on her like laying someone to sleep he used to gently carefully beat her to encourage the swelling glitches in her mind my grandmother is divorced now sometimes my father poisons her food sometimes my auntie breaks into her home and leaves all the doors unlocked most times she cries about her mother's death and the brother she hasn't seen in sixty years most times she squeezes kisses into us and farewells us with chewy mints or chocolate flavored goo

but my grandfather's step-mother well she's disgusting because she wants to own the deteriorating roof over her head her daughter is tarnishing the family name because "disgusting" married and divorced again "what idiot would take her she has no brains" her step-niece who refuses to be aware of tired humans; humans who are her family are only her concern to fling her tongue at I want to scream is it because she's had sex with three different men? which she may have not have as much as touched once haram she states haram she accuses haram she blinds herself with the word and forgets that her God forgives as much as she judges

بالتسليم بعض مش بنيز

Bizr

one crack on the molar and splitting with my teeth on my tongue the seed and spitting out the shell a light brown pile mimics the holy mountain that is my window view cracking sounds echo in a chaos of an orchestra around the room fresh watermelon leftovers fed to cows and sheep so that you can roast and entertain yourselves with its seeds crack crack in between hypocritical conversations "I hope the place you bought these doesn't sell cigarettes and alcohol" there is saliva on your fingers and your aim for the tray is weak instead the bizr decorating that UNICEF blanket covering your hundred dollar jeans while you're filling your mouth with entertainment and spitting out shells that fall to the ground as the bullets pierce your in-law's back / your daughter in-law didn't meet your criteria so instead you feed off making it hard for her to sleep I look from one person to the next as I hand them the small cup of mattee they're smiling at me but their eyes tell me they've shred my name through their sets of white teeth crack slurp hands wiping over their overfed bellies and momentarily resting their curious minds to have the audacity to pray and ask God to bring back the electricity to spy and prey on the lives of the very people they have within their company

The Olive Trees Are Watching

fluorescent trees in black seas as olives become pupils seeing leaves in a congested dabke to the rhythm of a winter breeze during a summer sleep and lights sprinkled in relief in a sky that is tired of the village's beliefs

عيد كل
ميلاد
سعيد

The Stolen Season

she breathed a cold breath and I smelled almond blossoms too early / the season was stolen from her and farmers wept before the sky finally did petrichor in waves above her grainy ocean of red and I had a little less to long for as the sun confused the wet petals but I understood this feeling well / she didn't quite know if she was where I came from or if I was only here to bid farewell

Old Bedsheets

"it's so cold and heavy" cold and heavy? "hmm" I'm going to write that down "what?" silence as death filled the room cloaking her like a costume she wore it unflatteringly it didn't fit right what's that smell? bang in the distance sprawled on the carpet I glanced back and my sheets cradled her as sleep borrowed her for another round

Dear Rose

we're awake in the AM when the sun is still on its knees tired of hoping for a better view of the world our eyes are mostly closed then and our lips open to let out all of what we have for each other they only close in front of others because the sun shines on them but not for them / for some reason everyone is always looking down creating shadows to see us through and sometimes I sigh for us but I know the sun has it worse we sleep until it starts calling for the moon until another day has already disappointed today / we woke in the PM but early enough to see the sun's tears through all of our closed curtains / it has been a mellow day so far a day of stretching out together on the couch I'm home alone now getting through procrastinated house work I've been thinking of you a lot lately and not as an afterthought my thoughts of you are like red coal coated in the ashes of my day-to-days / how is your mind? is your blood flowing uninterrupted? are your passions like a waterfall? is your smile genuine? does your bed rest your soul at night? today's thoughts are more specific like if I asked you to come would your childhood feelings be the wind beneath the plane's wings? would you come here and help me satisfy the sun on this side of the world? would the shadows roaming through the village split with the light we walk together? can you see past the shadows to remember those childhood feelings? can you make a bed here with me to really rest that tired soul?

When Breaths Touch

I have fingers just like before just as they've always been five fingers on each hand they often meet each other they're always meeting the air but never before have they breathed have they grown lungs that swell between your hair and a breath that touches the one escaping your lips

Mashqooq

where the dusty grey overwhelms its presence enough to respect the horizon that births mountains amongst flesh the taste of spice and floss that finds its way inside us and refuses to quench the ground so I find my ground inside you and you find my lips to share the ocean inside me

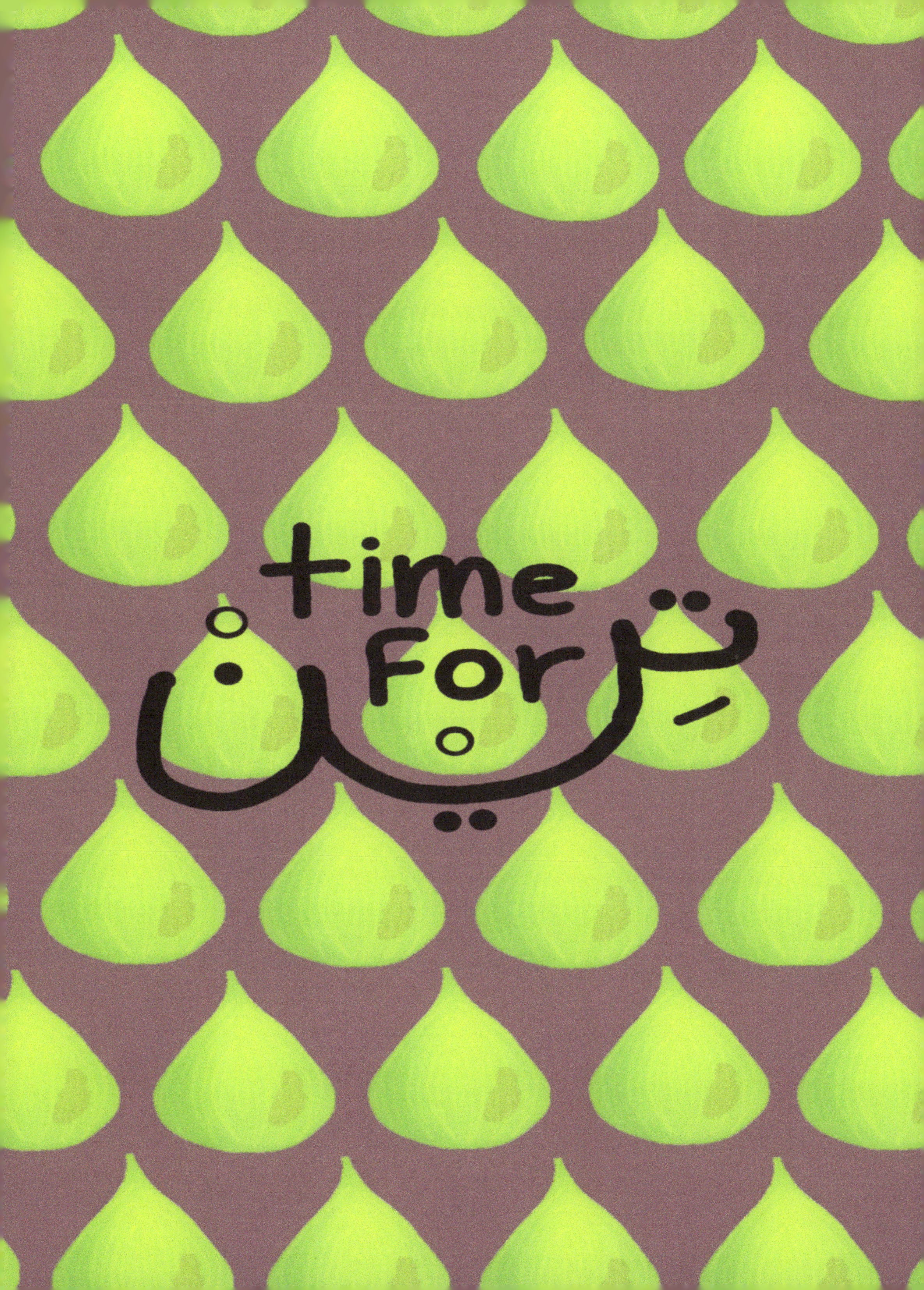
time for
تين

I travelled Away From Myself And Returned Away From Him

two hundred and thirty nine days faded within one desultory week / it ended on turning wheels I had my windows down as the breeze dabbed at my cheeks / the dalliance of rainfall had mostly withdrawn to hum to itself within the obscure romance of fugacious solitary in clouds / the fingers on my right hand were counted one by one by the steering wheel my mind assembled around an emollient to my nagging nostalgia / be calm be here becoming petrichor that claims me as part of this side of the world / I was a seed once that the first light caressed on this very soil and I was in Paris when I realised my individuality was the efflorescence of my soul my detached roots sang in breaths euphoniously back through me by virtue of dauntless kisses that talk to God on weekdays and speak of loving me everyday / a pyrrhic victory in my ears that dissociates from what my eyes since a week cannot perceive it and the phone rings while I catch rain on my cheek I catch it then I drive back home and sleep with it at night to the two hundred and thirty nine days of which his lingering redolence remains

Eating Shawarma Tastes Different When I'm Single

"Okay let's plan. What are we going to do?" It was a year-long separation that floated many unknowns and drowned many expectations. We dressed our emotions in poly-vinyl chloride and threw them into the ocean. I thought about my feelings being out of place and dolphins suffocating on plastic. I think he thought about me losing those feelings as they traveled across the seas. The oceans between us were lengthy and the year degraded into months slower than pvc did. The oceans swallowed the sun at all times of the day or the night and the moonlight sprinkled on the edge of their waves at all times of the day or the night. I'd say goodnight as his day started and I'd lose a breath to the oceans. I'd raise my voice at my mother and I'd lose a breath to the oceans. I'd defend his name and then be offended by his words — and I'd lose a breath to the oceans. I think I drained my lungs into the seas long before my tears made them saltier. When I finally began to float on a thin layer of air above the seas, I was a month away from claiming what the oceans had taken away from me. When the month turned into weeks I remembered the ocean hadn't taken anything. I had already been throwing myself into it, long before I met him. This side of the world was too large for me and the other too small. Yet I constantly thought about shawarma, amongst many other small things. "Okay let's plan. What are we going to do?" The question that multiplied as the countdown began to reach its end. The only things we could come up with were eating shawarma and ice cream together. Syria was too small for me but I crowded it with memories I pretended I wasn't attached to. This time all I cared about was spending a year with him within the month we had. And in turn none of my memories in Syria cared about me. Eating shawarma is different when I'm single. I wanted the shawarma guy to ask me if I was the daughter of Amed Richani and praise sharing my last name. I wanted to ask him to add extra chicken and pay him more and then ask for twenty shawarmas. I wanted the feeling of worrying about garlic mayo hanging on my lip in front of hundreds of people. I wanted to be met with a sky wild with stars as I wiped the garlic off my chin. I wanted to hear the honking of horns and our group of cousins unwinding to form a line. I wanted to sit on those steps behind the gate that pealed blue and white and had been welcoming us for a quarter of a century. Greasy shawarma wrapping that had been licked clean meant it was ice cream time at Mounir

Saimoua's shop. Amo Mounir always beamed as we crowded his shop and emptied his freezer. And someone would always say, "Don't forget vanilla ice cream for sito!" It was my grandmother's favourite. "Okay let's plan. What are we going to do?" We ate shawarma and we ate ice cream. I waited in the car alone and saw neither Amo Mounir nor the shawarma guy who was related to me. The shawarma was bland and I was full halfway through and the ice cream tasted like lactose and sugar. We ate both sitting in the Chevrolet and the only sounds I heard were the car's distinctive scraping metal on tar sound. I couldn't see the sky. I wanted to cry as I realized I was lost in the oceans inside me.

Can I Keep Him?

I have grown impatient with death death that not only narrates its own story but that of the living too and has love scared to trust itself inside me because death lingers in my rear view

National Anthem

different shades of absence overwhelms the tight space that I sit within twenty million individuals yet grouped as one you tell me how to shape my words yet they have a mind of their own my fingers only know as much as my mind chooses to acknowledge and the strings you strum upon your guitar speak the truth your country cannot bear to hear and I sit within four walls on a pivotal day with individuals who speak so little yet know so much and we are told femininity refuses comparison in the presence of a he and that he is weak in his degradation of women half your world is delicate hands worn out by an internal poison from fruitless seeds and soil that once raised families miscarries lives from the poison spilled from spoiled minds I know not what I see for what I feel is strangeness from familiar faces that once held my hand and now leave burning scars upon my skin accidents happen and yet you fail to acknowledge them as your own there are no roses that grow from barren ground and yet the thorns still pierce my skin

Roofs

tapping onto the four walls of the rusted khazan hearing the intro of a whisper only to catch debris from the wind that's passing through the areeshy from below / sunrise is too out of reach to be hearing Fairouz but it's a voiceless tune beating against familiar echoes

Shbiki

early conscious in a sea of green that unsettles within four walls where the floor is bare of migrating bags that are either packed with dust or tears or hope and constantly thrown into the clouds / sleep hurts when the clouds come back down with you and linger in the village absorbing all sound stealing enough breaths seeping into veins and lacing bitter coffee cups with contagious migraines and sweetened Arabic coffee goes cold though not as cold as the absence of the family who left it behind as cold as exhaling air from between their summer and winter and wedding and old jabal clothes the jabal had little sleep and 5am broke out borders within all of its children between their exhales and inhales and so dead air now meets each heartbeat fighting against flowing blood one two three fighting against distances as far as the ceiling from my lungs and I'm afraid to fill mine with air and have another be filled with one two three bullets that sometimes lie happily on wedding floors

Strange

the arrangement of letters made people cringe the sounds that bounced themselves in preparation for the words to be said wanted instead to bounce into a void my grandfather upon hearing this name shook his suddenly more wrinkled face and his only words were "these people are not for us" rumours were that this man's silhouette was recognised outside a home moments after a famous robbery took place in the village ridiculous sounding rumours pumped into my ears some reaching my mind and others just coating my eardrums a married man asking for women's hands' in marriage an abusive husband a disliked brother a repetitive tongue

initially his conversational style I disliked in a familiar way the way that I disliked most conversational discourse within the village this man had denied that he dyed his hair and the denial was strange because he was expressing negativity towards one dying his hair perhaps at his age? perhaps it was because of his gender? it was also strange because he was lying about something as simple as hair dye this man expressed a profound love towards me but his words were strange "I can't believe I finally have you I've been waiting for this moment to finally have you in our home no this is now your home and we're simply living in it" I did not want his home I did not want to be referred to his anything I had a name

soon after this man would be so ecstatic in my presence and he would express this by ordering me to get up and get lunch ready or to make some tea it was all strange but it was also a first experience a new experience was this normal behaviour in an abnormal society? his wife was also strange but in a different way in a way that she would simply shake her head if muddy boots decorated her clean carpet in a way that she would continue to pour tea when sunflower seed shells were thrown across the kitchen floor it was strange that she was to retrieve a cup of water when it wasn't for her this man and his wife would be doing the same nothing from the same distance from the tap was this a strange family? were they just strange to me? he would refer to his wife as woman more than he would use her name his voice was always raised when things were not his way until then I just thought it was strange a strange I did not like this family was poor in many ways and these many ways resulted in financial poverty no matter my life no matter my personality no matter my name I had "outsider" painted on my forehead using the black soot that coated the inside of the wejaq "outsider" mostly came with a financial status, one that danced along the higher end of the spectrum it was all untrue the reasons behind my stained forehead were my parents who indeed carried that status they also carried a combined seventy years of labour on their back under their eyes they carried a combined one hundred and twenty hours of trade a week their status came with shoulder problems with oil burns with no week-ends and pains to pass down to their children and so this wrongfully inherited status of mine had this man demanding money from me it also had him taking money off my grandfather who cannot stand him

those incidents were of the firsts to alter the feeling of strangeness to the sounds of alarm bells that went off in my head and travelled down my spine if I wanted to be more precise I unknowingly disliked this man before I heard about him before I heard his voice my sister spoke of a strange man invading her space and approaching her on the street to ask her about Australia and his sister in Australia this was the man I now know and wish I had no ties to he approached me once also asking for money but that time he wanted me to hide the incident from his son he wanted the money for something his son had told him not to pay for

this man is a husband and perhaps like many does not deserve the title visiting homes for the first time alone or with others has the dwellers asking of my marital status and to whom / the oldest living generation of the husband's family is what they target to express their opinions "his wife is good the poor thing dealt with a lot I guess plenty of people go through hard times" one home two homes, ten homes taxi drivers neighbours the arrangement of letters made people cringe

this man is a father and perhaps like many does not deserve the title he has a few extra years ahead of my father yet has not worked in ten years his children put a roof over their father's head and he placed struggles over his fourteen year-old son's head hard work draining work mentally exhausting work so that their father can disperse this hard work with his ego only leaving behind deep holes for those around him to fall into

love / when I could be true to the status enforced on me I expressed love in all the ways possible and one way was gifting I loved gifting I spent time on the gift I tried to trap as much emotion as one could into materials and passed them along to the one I love birthdays anniversaries celebrations simply as an expression of love I loved this man's son / his son's shoes his son's jacket his son's watch all on him and on the base of his son's shoes that he wore was my respect my love my mental ease

I could no longer see this man I felt as though looking into his eyes would make my own bleed the shark eyes my brother had described were hunting to make everything and anything his at everyone's and everything's expense he lied about hair dye he lies about countless things and one day he tried to make me lie to his son this lie also involved money this man asked me for money followed by asking of me to hide this exchange and the reason for it I feel as though my kindness is unacknowledged I feel as though I am an object I feel as though I am an exploited financial status that I do not meet and I now feel the desire for this man to disappear into a void

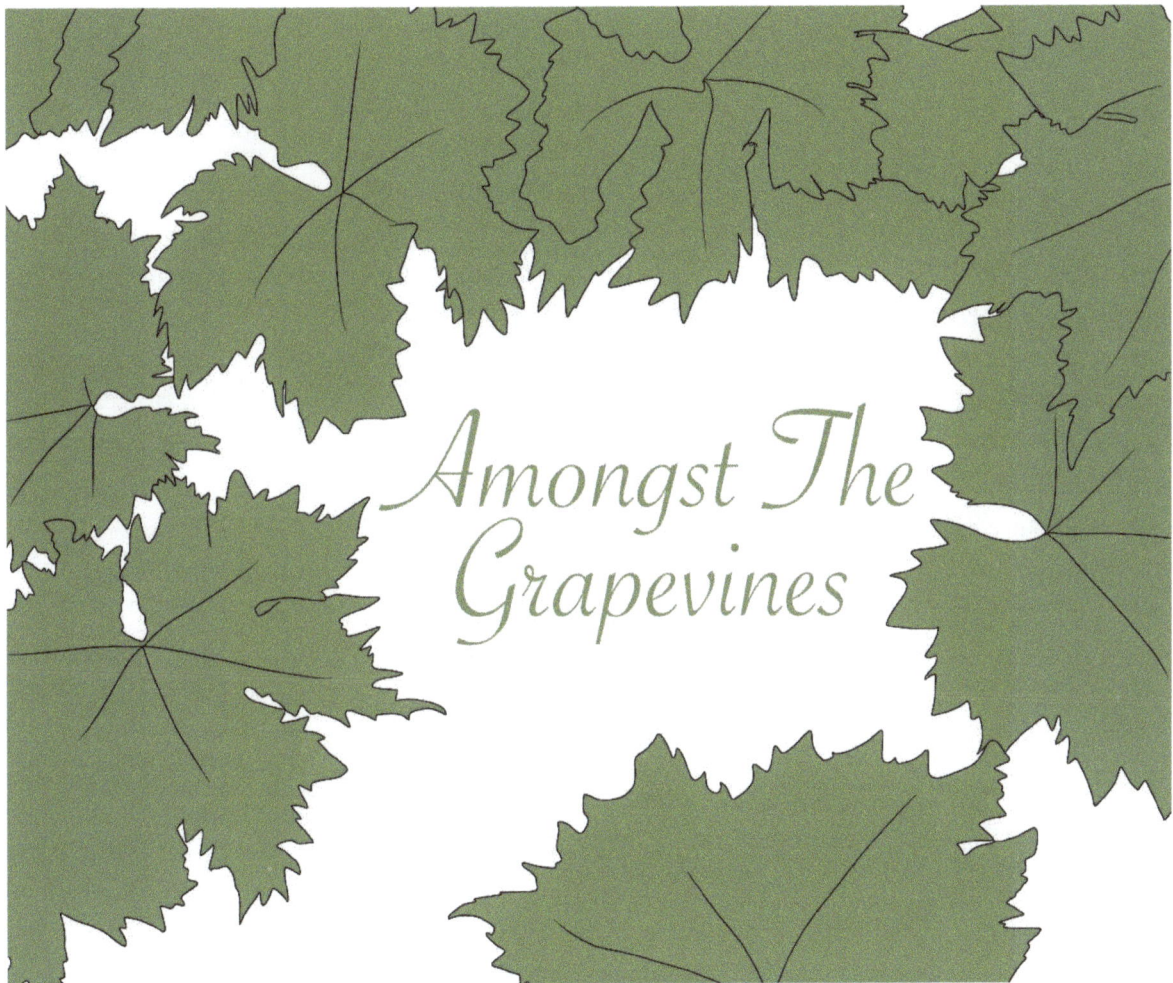

Amongst The Grapevines

National Anthem
(Instrumental)

I touched the inner side and you tore it all off of you the shadow doesn't recognise it's own flame the carpet is patterned with history in shades of red that give me anxiety and the music playing is telling me that it is the end / pillows lining the walls to match the number of children that once lived here where are they now? and who are we to be here? what more is there to do but to relax to the view of gas you're the only one to give the guitar strings the freedom they deserve and to cradle the instrument's body worshipping her curves she knows you she needs you share her with your motherland's wounds they need her she feels like dish-washed hands and her lips are crooked when she smiles please let it flood where flames aren't there onto all the flat roofs and take away the burning in my voice the fire doesn't recognise itself in my eyes

Blood Runs Too Deep It
Drowns You

crawl into darkness where crawlers feast feeding upon sadness where sad souls weep weeping rain upon skin where skin scars deep deep words lay heavy smothering in sleep sleeping away the sun where nights do bleed bleeding from the inside where death I need dying to smile where smiling lips do fake faking a love where lovers don't make making your fate where fate will devastate devastation in their hands where handled with care caring to see them yet they cared not I be there

Bodies In A Haystack

maybe if we collected a few pointed honey bodies with veiny thoughts from amongst needles in herds of silent roars swaying from our proximity in seconds too fast to breathe wouldn't it be easier than dusty storms of parties that part society in needles too invisible in blood too drinkable in beards too drenched in youth overcrowded basements with narratives too unfulfilled with epileptic frames / point and target at a magazine and release onto the page with a full chamber grasp pull back sharply and release the amount of words it takes to dismember a beating heart to raise children into the fiery ash you feared their adolescence would become in order to not become an artsy rubble shot too shook to not want to care

The In-between

I pull on draws too aggressively but they can take it I make out my reflection when I try too hard to avoid the mirror sometimes I know what I'm looking for sometimes my mind is tangled with recycled numbers that drip with wax trapped in a still of a recycled celebration wax that's trapped the thoughts of recycled people / number one has the most fun but recycled goods get tired it's never about getting older it's about getting more tired and number one is about hiding how tired you are / he was here first and sometimes I stumble upon him in draws raising frames to eyes that seem to shrink the more tired I get just like his did / I can never see through his lenses just like I rarely hear through his voice every few months I would try again anyway I liked how they felt resting behind my ears framing the tired beneath my eyes but I couldn't see they belonged to someone even more tired than me and sometimes I thought about the person he was when he wasn't the first to be there and it's always more about the recycled people and the recycled life that initiated his tired journey / clenched fists that only spread out across his mother's cheek skin that was too white tongues that could only twist and click certain ways southerners that only knew the west friends he couldn't claim the Middle East had a place here but it was a lonely space with its own tired pace his father spread it out on land a different shade of red than the one he had left / it made him dislike apricots they made his hands grow tired at eight there were no little trucks to clutch his hands instead fit around the wheel of a tractor there was always bread there was always milk but it was a life where there were always hungry kids it tore away hopes and dreams and in his teenage years placed a salt shaker in one hand and a frying basket in the other he has passed the basket on to someone else now and gone back to where he came from but it isn't where he has been he's watching his father recycle away the little breaths he has left / his daughters have learnt how to claim both shades of red and what they mean but perhaps he's tired because he doesn't know how to exist in the in-between

Loud Silences Bleed

one extended wing of embellished gold only causes harm floating on floral bed sheets with a song escaping a set of foreign lips I've been kissing / only the language turns the words into muffled words I hear like my screams beneath the seven seas that I've been blaming these past few years and then silence / the humming fridge type of silence / the wind escaping five metre high widows type of silence / the two beating hearts in different rhythms type of silence / the silence of knowing the ones who belong here are still asleep and the sun will warm their winter skies long before our summer sky sighs in its presence I hide my open hand beneath blossoms where no one would care to look and then I hear laughter that almost ripples the wetness coating my cheeks and then I hear my mother's voice telling me so

Guests

my branches were flakey and human contact was peeling them raw but yes I grew more branches from my bleeding fingertips / having people over was less filled with premature silences and more filled with words that echoed across flat roofs to be invited beneath a tiled one / tired words like an ultrasonic shrill being rediscovered recycled words fine tuned by deep voices and only used in a battle of the strength of conversation

Abdullah

twenty-three years spent like breaking a loaf of bread between ten and having it returned to me expectantly memorising the taste and obsessing over it only for my taste buds to suddenly meet paralysis / nice to meet you my blood bread and water that flows beneath the bridge and returns to its name the name that fed me loved me and raised me and yet I cannot call my own / nice to meet you the breaking of silence that leaves crumbs all over the floor that degrade before they rot and replenish the steps we take towards an unknown that brightens with everyday that shortens your absence / nice to meet you for the first time since unmet expectations ravel and wisdom grew from the tears that reached your jawline and flour remained undusted from your beard / nice to meet you Abdullah

Loghat

barking dogs and barking motorcycles and YouTube videos on Facebook pages that let us know the things we already know and never learn from I can only get by in this language I can only express love in mundane words in this language and I have to listen in frustrated sighs when I translate my words into this language and then I silence both languages to fill blue and white porcelain with two different types of olives and the tomatoes of the mountain and the cucumbers that belong more in my uncle's fruit and veggie shop than here and the scrambled eggs I do not eat and the laban that now confuses me and the zaatar I never used to eat and now my palate craves and the Lebanese bread that might be too old / I fill the porcelain plates and bowls and I wait / I wait as Facebook is scrolled through I wait and I hear them say something that means "okay" / I wait and then my waiting is short-lived as my short fuse shortens my relationship with the only reason I think this other language is more important than my own

Drought

split the ocean in half and walk through desert land / the betrayal of water has the
ground splitting beneath exposed skin splitting exposed skin leaving it rough against
white linen and leaving it rubbed by fingertips that know its path too well I wonder if
lips split when they say my country's name and this thought convinces me which side
of the ocean I would rather envelop me

United We Stand And Either Way I Fall

one two three four five foam mattresses covered in a layer of plastic that dust covers that breaths cover that summer heat and winter frost cover that hands don't cover except once every two or three or four years that suitcases occasionally meet when they're empty and say goodbye when they're full but then one two empty suitcases stay and one two breaths continue to escape and one two voices sometimes become silence and one two aren't enough to count the one two days that have passed in plastic covering the one two souls in one two three four five painful words that are too much for one two under one roof "I don't love you anymore"

Roots

painting your leaves of constantly fading different shadings of flawless green mistaking basing gratification on unlawful adaptations to mainstream societal ideals

altabe' yaghleb altatabo'

embrace
your
roots

drop the paintbrush you painfully disfigured from yourself and use the storm of fury and rejection from society to rain down and flourish the depth of your accent

Racist Rice

I don't wash it excessively for yabraq perhaps just once tipping out the excess diluted milky pigmentation of water until the droplets are falling at an agitating pace every grain plumps up with heat you see so the collection laying in my palm could be a handful a couple of spoonfuls I've saved from sliding through tubes along with Morning Fresh and mush just a quick glance at the sink the aluminium highlighting numerous white rods helpless to do nothing but slip through the gaps between my fingers and dance around above a wet layer just a quick glance long enough to utter God forgives before blasting the tap and draining them a short enough time to disallow any guilt to settle and time and time again traditional dishes after the next; wash drain waste yabraq, kousa mehshi or as a side with kafta and tabouli feeding the drains instead of millions of hungry mouths that have almost forgotten how rice tastes

Craving كوسى

Almond

even spring is late in its wake taking a weak deeper into winter's bitterness and all the strength is only for those who raised almond trees and are called upon by singing birds in the undressed AM when exposed legs remain not judged by the young sun waiting for the rays to grow into something the small white blossoms can use to smile back at me as I wait for the expected chill of the reminder of your absence from my touch and the reminder that it's not time to reveal what winter forces me to conceal a colour scheme undecided by the dark sky of the night through the pain the window's glass may cause if it was to be the farewell I'd choose but I'm curious if this so-called spring morning will expose a feeling other than the colour of bruise I feel / AM is too broad a concept so I sit by at a lower angle for a higher chance to decide if sunrise is what I'm looking for and nothing more than to bathe in it's empathy of obscure existence and it's early weakness still asks of me to close my eyes a couple of days for the new season to flourish and void it's insecurities of fragmentation and a couple of hours for the darkness to no longer hold onto me and allow me to smell the almond blossoms before the village's first aware breath meets my neck

Index

Reviews

"As someone who comes from a family of immigrants, this book resonated with me to the core. Composed of both short stories and poetry, this collection explores every crevice of a mind split in between two worlds.I felt all of Richani's words in my bones. The stories she tells are as vibrant as memories - by the end of the book, I'd lived a hundred different lives, each one as important and impactful as the other. Her words encapsulate someone whose life is split in different countries, memories, cultures, the confusion and multitudes that is diaspora."

— Hinnah Mian, author of To Build A Home

"Richani's Amongst the Grape Vines is textural; the language demands the reader's attention, drawing them in to description made tangible. The writing moves seamlessly between the beautifully sensual microscopic and the overwhelming macroscopic, painting a stunning and immersive view of Richani's lived experience of Syria. Each essay or poem exacts its emotions from the reader with precision— this book is beautiful, nuanced, and well worth the read."

— Sarah "Sam" Saltiel, author of A Thesaurus for the Way Water Returns

"This book gripped me. From the first sentence I read, it gripped me. The way Richani weaves in and out of scenes and images feels almost dream-like, and what you are left with long after is not only a memory of her striking words, but the memory of the emotions Richani transfers to you through her intricately-woven lines. Her style is such that each passage, exploring a separate yet interwoven theme, builds up until its final lines, which will strike you deeply and will remain in the pit of your stomach. Amongst the Grapevines explores not only the context and effects of direct violence, but also the violence of apathy, the violence of ignorance, and the varied experiences of inter- personal violence that can arise between others. Beyond this, Richani also shines light on the beauty, kindness, and love there is to be found in humanity and in connecting with one's roots, as all sides - both light and dark - of this multifaceted collection compose Richani's reconnection with her own roots. At times this connection to the land of Syria is quite literal, as she connects with the red earth of her country, the grapevines, and the olive trees which, as she states, "are watching" - watching as tur- moil unfolds and as humanity is pitted against itself; and, from this place of reflection, Richani, along with the olive trees, can critique in the brushstrokes of her beautiful syllables, the context she grapples to understand around her - critiques ranging from the most intimate of levels to the most grand and abstracted, but all seamlessly inter- woven. Minney Richani brings to us a complex and rich portrait of her Syria - the Syria she knows, the Syria she wishes to know, and the Syria she carries with her in her heart as a member of its diaspora. Filled with both heartache, hope, and ultimately a pressing message for others to care, to look, to listen, and to love, this is not a book to be missed."

— Ava Balis, author of Have You Ever Been Mine?

Acknowledgement of Previous Publication

Eating Shawarma Tastes Different When I'm Single
    First Published in 1701 Press issue 4 of is this up

Loghat
    First Published in 1701 Press issue 4 of is this up

Mama's Hair Still Curls, Mine Doesn't
    First published in Poetry Diversified 2019

Racist Rice
    First published in Poetry Diversified 2018

Red Earth
    First published in Bacopa Literary Review

Sito
    First published in Jabalna Issue 1

Spoils of War
    First published in Poetry Diversified 2019

Strange
    First published in Riza Multimedia Poetry and Art Journal

Syria, no not that Syria
    First published in Lane Cove Literary Awards 2017: An Anthology
    Published on Lemon Theory
    Published in Jabalna Issue 0
    Aired on OutsideIn 4EB Radio

The In-Between
    First published in Queensland University of Technology Literary Salon 2020 Collection
    Published on GetYourz Radio Blog

The Mohamad Boys
    First published in Questions Online Journal Issue 08
    Published in Climate Health and Courage – Future Leaders

Traversing Affairs
    First Published in Lane Cove Literary Awards 2016: An Anthology

United We Stand and Either Way I Fall
    First published in Poetry Diversified 2019

Glossary of Arabic Terms

Altabe' yaghleb altatabo' - the nature overrides the nurture

Areeshy - grapevine

Bizr - seeds

Dabke - a dance performed by holding hands, linking arms or both holding hands and linking arms while moving in an open ended circle, by a repeated two steps to the right followed by a kick of the right foot. Another version of the Dabke is instead taking one step to the right, one step to the left followed by the kick of the right foot. The person leading the Dabke is referred to as the head and they usually get creative with the footwork, think spicy lunges, squats and star jumps. Sometimes they leave the Dabke all together to face the rest of the dancers

Dar - household

Haram - religiously impermissible. Also used to express sympathy or sadness for another, such as in, "ya haram, because of her circumstances she's unable to visit Syria." The term is also commonly misused to replace Eib, meaning socially shameful/ unacceptable

Jabal - mountain, also refers to the city of Swaida/the Druze region

Jido - grandfather

Kafta - mince meat (lamb or beef) mixed in with parsley, tomato, onion, garlic, salt, black pepper, nutmeg, allspice, coriander, ginger, cinnamon, clove, and olive oil and pressed into a deep dish tray. Topped with slices of potato, onion, tomato and baked

Khawati Hayati - my sisters, my life. This refers to my mother and her four sisters and what they refer to one another. This is also the name of their group chat on WhatsApp

Khazan - a metal water/fuel tank

Kousa Mehshi - the same mix as in the yabraq but instead stuffed into zucchinis and cooked in a tomato soup or a turmeric yoghurt soup

Loghat - languages

Makdoos - tiny eggplants stuffed with walnuts, garlic, capsicum, salt and pickled in olive oil

Motreb - Singer

Shawarma - a Lebanese bread wrap containing garlic spread, pickles and chicken sliced off a sheesh (skewer) marinated in cumin paprika black pepper cinnamon, lemon juice, salt, garlic, black pepper and olive oil (yoghurt? White vinegar? What about the lamb shawarma?)

Sito - grandmother

Tabouli - a salad made up of finely chopped parsley, shallots and tomatoes, mixed in with fine bulgar, lemon juice, olive oil, salt and black pepper

Wejaq - a warmer, made of iron which also serves as a stove with a rectangular surface and a mini oven. It runs on either diesel or wood fire and is usually assembled in the centre of a room with pipes running up, along, all over ceilings/walls and out of a window or through a wall. Sometimes a gust of wind pushes back through the pipes causing it to "afet" and results in black ash covering every surface of the room. This is sometimes followed by tears

Yabraq - a mix of short grain rice, parsley, tomato, onion, garlic, salt, black pepper, nutmeg, allspice, coriander, ginger, cinnamon, clove, lemon juice and olive oil wrapped in grape vine leaves. Varrying versions of this are also known as waraq eneb, yalange, dolma and dolmades

Yallah - derived from Ya Allah meaning oh God and mostly used as hurry up. Also meaning oh well, oh yeah! and I'm a non Arab when I find out you're Arab

Zaatar - a mix of dried oregano, sesame seeds, toasted Lebanese bread, sumac and salt

Laban - yoghurt

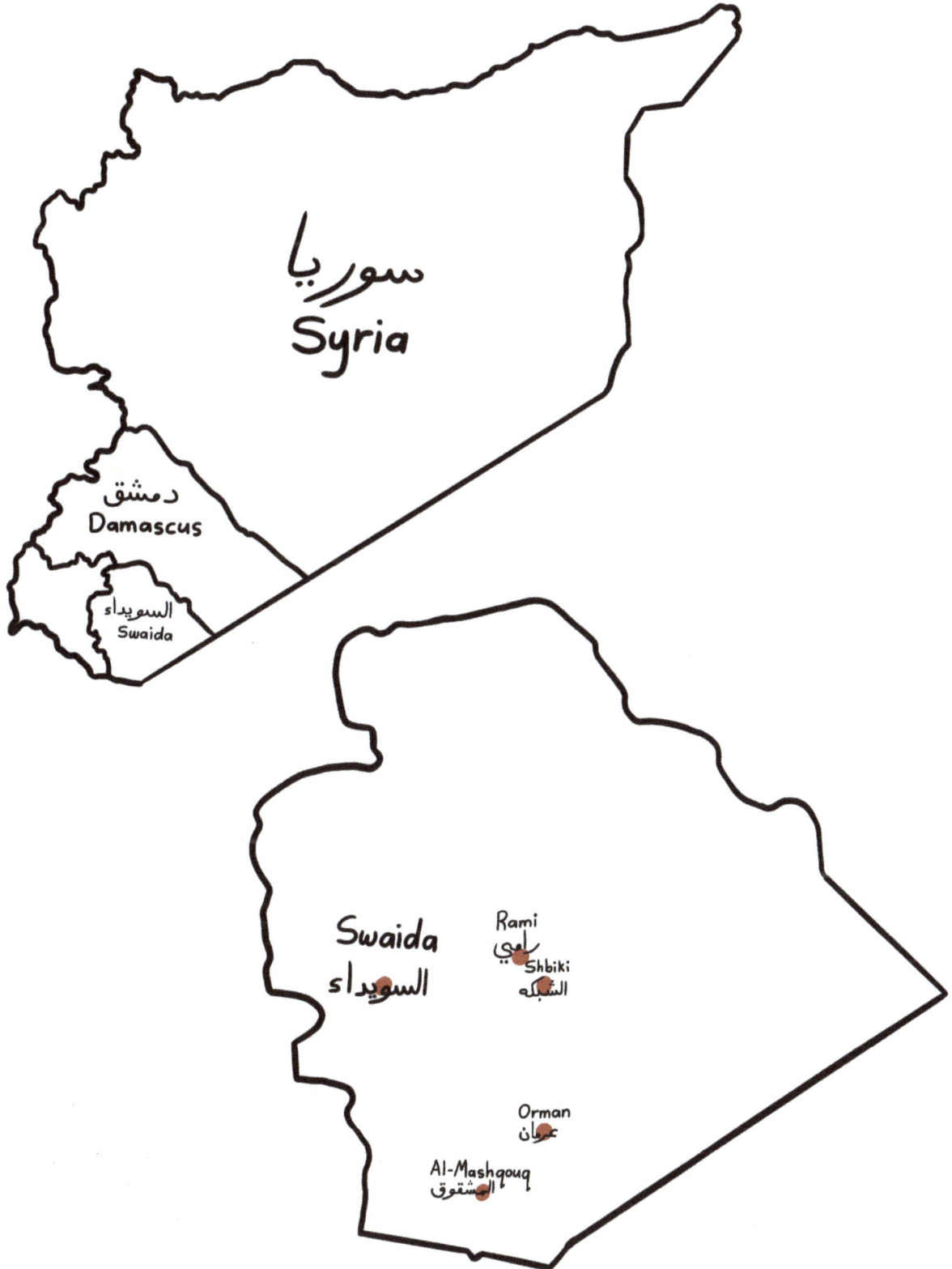

سوريا
Syria

دمشق
Damascus

السويداء
Swaida

Swaida
السويداء

Rami
رامي
Shbiki
الشبكه

Orman
عمان

Al-Mashqouq
المشقوق